Christianity, Cults & Religions Leader Guide

Paul Carden

This Leader Guide accompanies the

Christianity, Cults & Religions 6-Session DVD-Based Study
(ISBN 9781596364134 or 9781596364271)

with

Christianity, Cults & Religions Participant Guide
(ISBN 9781596364295)

**Containing: Glossary of Words, Definitions of Concepts,
Activity Sheets, Charts**

© 2010 Bristol Works, Inc.
Rose Publishing, Inc.
4733 Torrance Blvd., #259
Torrance, California 90503 U.S.A.
Email: info@rose-publishing.com
www.rose-publishing.com

Celtic cross photo ©Pears2295

Scripture quotations marked "NASB" are taken from the *New American Standard Bible*, © Copyright 1960, 1962, 1963, 1968, 1971, 1972, 1973, 1975, 1977, 1995 by The Lockman Foundation. Used by permission.
Scripture quotations marked "NIV" are taken from the *Holy Bible, New International Version*®. NIV®. Copyright © 1973, 1978, 1984 by International Bible Society. Used by permission of Zondervan. All rights reserved.

Printed in the United States of America

Contents

About the Complete Christianity, Cults & Religions DVD-Based Kit

(ISBN 9781596364134)

The Kit includes everything you need to teach *Christianity, Cults & Religions*, using professionally-produced video sessions and a PowerPoint® presentation. The Complete Kit includes:

- DVD with 6 teaching sessions

- One printed *Christianity, Cults & Religions Participant Guide* (ISBN 9781596364295)

- One printed *Christianity, Cults & Religions Leader Guide* (ISBN 9781596364288) + PDF Leader Guide

- One printed *Rose Bible Basics: Christianity, Cults & Religions* handbook (ISBN 9781596362024)

- One *Christianity, Cults & Religions* pamphlet comparing 20 religions and cults side by side (ISBN 9789901981403)

- *Christianity, Cults & Religion* PowerPoint® presentation on CD-ROM (ISBN 9781890947323)

- PDF files for posters, fliers, handouts and bulletin inserts for promotion

Available at www.ChristianityCultsandReligions.com or
www.rose-publishing.com, or by calling Rose Publishing at
1-800-532-4278. Also available wherever good Christian books are sold.

About This Study

As Christians living in the 21st century, we are faced with increasing religious diversity and religious competition. In this ever-shrinking world, people in cults and other religions may be showing up on your doorstep, at your job, or maybe even in your own family. You might be wondering, How can I possibly "always be prepared to give an answer" (1 Peter 3:15)?

We should take our cue from the apostle Paul who skillfully employed his knowledge of pagan philosophies to evangelize unbelievers (Acts 17:16–34). To witness in today's world, Christians need a basic understanding of what cults and religions teach, so they can know how to relate to people in various religious groups.

In this study, Paul Carden explains the essential teachings of popular cults and major religions. But he also takes you beneath the surface to shed light on what really attracts and keeps people in these religious groups. Each session lays out a solid Scriptural foundation for discerning the truth and dispels common misconceptions and stereotypes. But above all, this study is here to help you think biblically, so you can evangelize with compassion, clarity, and confidence.

This study is designed for six 60-minute sessions with the video portion lasting 25–35 minutes and the group discussion lasting 15–25 minutes depending on the time allotted. You can expand the teaching to six 90-minute sessions with activities such as the Key Bible Verses, Quick Quiz, or the *Christianity, Cults & Religions* PowerPoint® presentation which includes other religions and cults not covered in-depth in the DVD.

About the Author

For more than 30 years, Paul Carden has been a leading researcher of religions, cults, and new religious movements. For six years, he co-hosted the live, nationwide *Bible Answer Man* radio broadcast alongside Ron Rhodes, Robert M. Bowman Jr., and other noted apologists. He joined Christian Research Institute and was the director of International Outreach under its founder, Walter Martin. He has also served as a senior editor of the *Christian Research Journal* and has spent six years as a missionary in Brazil.

Today he is the executive director of the Centers for Apologetics Research, an organization that monitors and researches religions and cults around the world. His passion for evangelism and educating Christians is evident. He brings to this study his extensive experience in training believers how to effectively witness to people in cults and world religions.

He and his wife, Lisa, have four children and live in San Juan Capistrano, California.

Definitions, Discernment, and Defending the Faith

Session 1 Outline
Definitions, Discernment, and Defending the Faith

1. Scriptural foundation

   a. Matthew 28:19

   b. Jude 3–4

   c. Matthew 24:4–5, 11, 24

   d. Acts 20:28–31a

   e. 2 Corinthians 11:3–4

   f. Galatians 1:6, 9

2. Practical definitions

   a. What is a religion?

   b. What is a cult?

   c. What is a heresy?

3. Six categories of false teaching:

   a. Revelation

   b. God – dangerous distortions about the true God

   c. Jesus Christ – deny Itus Lordship,

   d. Salvation – Cults teach legalism

   e. The church

   f. The future – Cults make false predictions

4. Why are people drawn into cults?

    a. The tactics used to recruit, convert, and hold members — *their bag of tricks*

    b. The personal vulnerability of the potential recruit

        myth - only misfits & losers join cults!

        • Proverbs 27:7; 14:12

5. How can we respond? *Some respond with ignorance*

    a. Have a mature grasp of Scripture

        • Hebrews 5:14; Ephesians 4:14

    b. Be vigilant

        • 1 Thessalonians 5:21–22

        • 1 John 4:1

        • Acts 17:11

    c. Practice caring outreach *to those caught in cults*

        • 2 Timothy 2:25

Key Terms

Religion "A set of beliefs that answers the ultimate questions. What is ultimate reality? What is the nature of the world? What is the nature of humanity? What is humanity's primary problem? What happens after death?" (Dean Halverson, *The Illustrated Guide to World Religions*; Bethany, 2003; p. 10)

"Any socially organized pattern of beliefs and practices concerning ultimate meaning that assumes the existence of the supernatural." (Rodney Stark, quoted in Irving Hexham, *Concise Dictionary of Religion*; IVP, 1993; p. 187)

Heresy "A teaching which directly opposes the essentials of the Christian faith, so that true Christians must divide themselves from all those who hold it." (Robert M. Bowman, Jr., *Orthodoxy and Heresy: A Biblical Guide to Doctrinal Discernment*; Baker, 1992; p. 50) *we cannot have fellowship with someone who affirms a heresy.*

"It is a Trojan horse, a means of establishing (whether by accident or design) an alternative belief system within its host. Heresy appears to be Christian, but it is actually an enemy of faith that sows the seed of faith's destruction." (Alister McGrath, *Heresy: A History of Defending the Truth*; HarperOne, 2009; p. 34)

Cult "An ideological organization held together by charismatic relationships *Extraordinary force of personality* and demanding total commitment." (Benjamin Zablocki, quoted in Herbert L. Rosedale and Michael D. Langone, *"On Using the Term 'Cult'"*) *which opens the door for manipulation + exploitation*

"A religious group originating as a heretical sect and maintaining fervent commitment to heresy." (Robert M. Bowman, Jr., *Orthodoxy and Heresy: A Biblical Guide to Doctrinal Discernment*; Baker, 1992; p. 115)

A cult of Christianity would be "a group of people, which claiming to be Christian, embraces a particular doctrinal system taught by an individual leader, group of leaders, or organization, which [system] denies (either explicitly or implicitly) one or more of the central doctrines of the Christian faith." (Alan Gomes as quoted in Ron Rhodes, *The Challenge of the Cults and New Religions*; Zondervan, 2001; p. 22)

Before the Session

ℭ *Prepare:*

- Ask God for guidance and pray for each participant.

- Watch DVD Session 1 on your own.

- See *Additional Resources* for further study.

- Read *Rose Bible Basics: Christianity, Cults & Religions* handbook chapters 1 and 7.

ℭ *Materials needed for this session:*

- DVD Session 1

- Bible

- Paper and pen for participants to write their contact information on.

- "What the Bible Teaches" section in *Christianity, Cults & Religions* PowerPoint® presentation (optional)

Opening the Session (15 minutes)

Use the *Did You Know?* facts to get participants thinking about today's topic. If you have a projector or whiteboard you can display the facts as participants enter the classroom. You can also read the facts aloud to the group before watching the DVD.

Did You Know?

How some groups answer these questions:

WHO IS GOD?
- God was a human who progressed to Godhood *(Mormonism)*
- God is the unknowable Allah *(Islam)*
- Every human being is God *(New Age)*
- God is an unnecessary concept *(Buddhism)*

WHO IS JESUS?
- A guru and ascended master *(New Age)*
- Michael the archangel *(Jehovah's Witnesses)*
- Lucifer's brother *(Mormonism)*
- One of Allah's honored prophets *(Islam)*

HOW ARE WE SAVED?
- By reaching a state of non-existence *(Buddhism)*
- Entering eternal life requires secret temple rituals *(Mormonism)*
- By being absorbed into Brahman *(Hinduism)*

When everyone gathers together, welcome participants and open the session in prayer. If you do not have participants' contact information, pass around a paper and pen for participants to write down their name, phone number, and/or e-mail address. Ask participants to introduce themselves to the group, and share why they joined this study and what they hope to gain from it.

❦ Introduce participants to the purposes of this study:

- To help you think biblically about cults and religions.

- To help you identify, understand, and answer people in other religions and cults.

- To help you to evangelize with clarity, conviction, and confidence.

Watch the DVD SESSION 1 (25 minutes)

- Note: Session 1 begins with a 4-minute introduction to the Christianity, Cults & Religions series.

- Refer class members to the session outline in their Participant Guides for note taking.

Group Discussion (15 minutes)

If the class is large, divide participants into small groups. If time allows, have a spokesperson from each small group share with the rest of the class some of the insights discussed in their group. (These questions are also located in the Participant Guide.)

1. Why is it important for Christians to learn about other religions? *we can be more effective in Sharing the Gospel*

2. What is discernment? And how does a Christian grow in discernment?

3. What does it mean to "defend the faith"? Give some examples of what defending the faith might look like.

4. After watching the first session, what are you excited about learning in this study?

5. What questions do you still have about this study?

Expand the Teaching (Optional – 30 minutes)

To expand the session to 90 minutes use one or more of the following activities. (Activity sheets for participants are located in the Participant Guide.)

- **KEY BIBLE VERSES** This study in Scripture can be completed individually or in small groups.

- **QUICK QUIZ** The quiz is based on the content in the DVD session, so you will want to have participants complete it only after watching the DVD.

- **PRESENTATION** Cover "What the Bible Teaches" section in *Christianity, Cults & Religions* PowerPoint® presentation.

Reaching Out (5 minutes)

℘ *Encourage participants to reflect on these questions throughout the week:*

1. How do I practice discernment in my spiritual life?

2. What can I do to learn how to better defend the faith?

3. Whom do I know that may be falling prey to false beliefs or getting involved in a cultic group? How should I speak with them? How should I pray for them?

(These questions are also found in the Participant Guide.)

℘ *Close the session in prayer.*

Key Bible Verses

MATTHEW 7:15–20

"Beware of the false prophets, who come to you in sheep's clothing, but inwardly are ravenous wolves. You will know them by their fruits. Grapes are not gathered from thorn bushes nor figs from thistles, are they? So every good tree bears good fruit, but the bad tree bears bad fruit. A good tree cannot produce bad fruit, nor can a bad tree produce good fruit. Every tree that does not bear good fruit is cut down and thrown into the fire. So then, you will know them by their fruits." *NASB*

Q What does Jesus warn us about? And how can we recognize danger?

A **False prophets who appear safe on the outside, but are actually looking to devour. We can identify them by the results of their actions and teachings.**

1 JOHN 4:1–4

"Beloved, do not believe every spirit, but test the spirits to see whether they are from God, because many false prophets have gone out into the world. By this you know the Spirit of God: every spirit that confesses that Jesus Christ has come in the flesh is from God; and every spirit that does not confess Jesus is not from God; this is the spirit of the antichrist, of which you have heard that it is coming, and now it is already in the world. You are from God, little children, and have overcome them; because greater is He who is in you than he who is in the world." *NASB*

Q How does John assure believers that they can resist being deceived?

A **He gives us a way to test the spirits—see what they teach about who Jesus is. Believers need not be afraid because we are God's children and God is greater than the one who is in the world.**

2 TIMOTHY 2:24–26

"The Lord's bond-servant must not be quarrelsome, but be kind to all, able to teach, patient when wronged, with gentleness correcting those who are in opposition, if perhaps God may grant them repentance leading to the knowledge of the truth, and they may come to their senses and escape from the snare of the devil, having been held captive by him to do his will." *NASB*

Q According to this passage, what should we do about those who oppose sound teaching?

A **Understand that they have been trapped by the devil. Gently correct them and desire that God would grant them repentance and lead them to the truth.**

Quick Quiz   ANSWER KEY (Answers in Bold)

1. According to the session, what is heresy?

    a. Teachings found in the Christian creeds.
    b. **Teachings that oppose the essentials of the Christian faith.**   *& undermines (Christian Faith*
    c. Any teaching not contained in a church's statement of faith.
    d. Anything I disagree with.

2. True or False? The people who join cults are usually social misfits with little education and have difficulty holding a job. **FALSE (This is a myth. Many people in cults are successful, intelligent, and talented.)**

3. According to this session, what draws people into cults?

    a. Looking for solace during an emotionally vulnerable time in life.
    b. The "love" they feel from cult leaders.
    c. The false promises that cult leaders make.
    d. (a) and (b)
    e. **All of the above**

4. True or False? Cults often use Christian vocabulary, but redefine the terms to mean something very different. **TRUE (This is the language barrier Christians often face when talking with people in cults.)**

5. According to this session, the four points derived from Jude 3–4 are: (1) There is one faith; (2) That faith is unchanging; (3) We are to earnestly contend for the faith; and (4) The faith has __**enemies (or adversaries)**__.

Additional Resources

ℭ Books

The Battle Belongs to the Lord: The Power of Scripture for Defending Our Faith by K. Scott Oliphint (P&R, 2003)

By Hook or by Crook: How Cults Lure Christians by Harold Busséll (McCracken, 1993)

Charts of Cults, Sects, and Religious Movements by H. Wayne House (Zondervan, 2000)

Correcting the Cults: Expert Responses to Their Scripture Twisting by Norman L. Geisler and Ron Rhodes (Baker, 2005)

Cults and the Occult by Edmond C. Gruss (P&R, 2002)

The Discipline of Spiritual Discernment by Tim Challies (Crossway, 2007)

Cults in Our Midst: The Hidden Menace in our Everyday Lives by Margaret Thaler Singer with Janja Lalich (Jossey-Bass, 1995)

Faith Has Its Reasons: Integrative Approaches to Defending the Christian Faith by Kenneth D. Boa and Robert M. Bowman, Jr. (Paternoster, 2005)

A Guide to New Religious Movements by Ronald Enroth, ed. (IVP, 2005)

Heresy: A History of Defending the Truth by Alister McGrath (HarperOne, 2009)

On Guard: Defending Your Faith with Reason and Precision by William Lane Craig (Cook, 2010)

Orthodoxy & Heresy: A Biblical Guide to Doctrinal Discernment by Robert M. Bowman, Jr. (Baker, 1992)

Scripture Twisting: Twenty Ways the Cults Misread the Bible by James W. Sire (IVP, 1980)

ℭ Internet

Apologetics Index   www.apologeticsindex.com

Apologetics Resource Center   www.arcapologetics.org

Be Thinking   www.bethinking.org

Centers for Apologetics Research   www.thecenters.org

Christian Apologetics & Research Ministry   www.carm.org

Institute for Religious Research   www.irr.org

Lee Strobel   www.leestrobel.com

Probe Ministries   www.probe.org

Ravi Zacharias International Ministries   www.rzim.org

Reasoning from the Scriptures Ministries   www.ronrhodes.org

Stand to Reason   www.str.org

Watchman Fellowship   www.watchman.org

The inclusion of a work or web site does not necessarily mean endorsement of all its contents or of other works by the same author(s) or organization.

Essential Christian Doctrine

Session 2 Outline
Essential Christian Doctrine

1. The standard

   a. General revelation (nature)

      • Psalm 19

      • Romans 1:20

   b. Special revelation (Scripture)

      • 2 Peter 1:21

      • 2 Timothy 3:16

2. Heresy and orthodoxy

   a. Heresy

   b. Orthodoxy

3. Four universal creeds

   a. Apostles' Creed

   b. Nicene Creed

   c. Athanasian Creed

   d. Definition of Chalcedon

4. A dozen essential doctrines

   a. God's unity

      • Deuteronomy 6:4

      • 1 Corinthians 8:5–6

   b. The Trinity

      • 2 Thessalonians 1:2

      • John 1:1

      • Matthew 28:19

c.   Human depravity

- Romans 3:9–20

- John 3:3

d.   The virgin birth

- Luke 1:34–35, Matthew 1:18

e.   The sinlessness of Christ

- Hebrews 4:15

- 1 Peter 2:22

- 2 Corinthians 5:21

f.   Christ's deity...

g.   ...and Christ's humanity

- John 1:14

- Hebrews 1:1–8

- Galatians 4:4–5

- 1 John 4:2–3

h.   God's grace

- Romans 5:10

- Titus 3:5

i.   Faith

- Ephesians 2:8–9

j.   Christ's atoning death

- Romans 3:25–26

k.   Jesus' bodily resurrection

- 1 Corinthians 15:1–6

l.   Christ's second coming

- Acts 1:11

- Revelation 1:7

Key Terms

Confession   (from Latin *confiteri*, "acknowledge") Like creeds, confessions are an active acknowledgement of the church's faith and teachings. "Confessions of faith" often include both creedal declarations and statements summarizing the distinctive teachings of a particular denomination or group of believers.

Creed   (from Latin *credo*, "I believe") A simple summary of beliefs. Creeds are easy to memorize and flexible to teach.

Doctrine   (from Latin *doctrina*, "teaching," "learning") A belief that a group holds as true. Christian doctrines organize and explain the beliefs the church learns from the Bible.

Heresy   (from Greek *hairesis*, "choice," "faction") A teaching that contradicts another teaching that has been accepted as the norm; the opposite of orthodoxy.

Orthodoxy   (from Greek *ortho*, "straight," and *doxa*, "belief, opinion") The opposite of heresy. Irenaeus (AD 130–200) used the word orthodox to characterize his own teachings, with which most other Church Fathers agreed, and the word heresy to define those of his adversaries. When Orthodox is capitalized (as in Greek Orthodox, Russian Orthodox) it refers to the church bodies of Eastern Europe and the Middle East that divided from the churches aligned with Rome in the Great Schism of AD 1054.

Before the Session

ℭ *Prepare:*

- Ask God for guidance and pray for each participant.

- Watch DVD Session 2 on your own.

- Review *Where Did the Creeds Come From?* and *The Apostles' Creed* on the following pages.

- See *Additional Resources* for further study.

ℭ *Materials needed for this session:*

- DVD Session 2

- Bible

- A copy of *The Apostles' Creed* for each participant (optional)

- "Christianity" section of *Christianity, Cults & Religions* PowerPoint® presentation (optional)

Opening the Session (5 minutes)

As participants enter, display this quote on a whiteboard or projector screen: "In essentials, unity. In nonessentials, liberty. And in all things, charity."— Peter Meiderlin, 17th-century Christian theologian

When everyone gathers, welcome participants and open the session in prayer. If your group has new participants, you may want to briefly cover the purposes of this study (see Session 1).

Watch the DVD   Session 2 (25 minutes)

- Refer class members to the session outline in their Participant Guides for note taking.

Group Discussion (25 minutes)

If the class is large, divide participants into small groups. If time allows, have a spokesperson from each small group share with the rest of the class some of the insights discussed in their group. (These questions are also located in the Participant Guide.)

1. Which essential doctrines do you think are easiest for people to accept? Which ones are most difficult? Why?

2. Which essential doctrines do you notice cults denying or distorting most often?

3. How does understanding the "bad news" of human depravity help us appreciate the "good news" of Jesus Christ?

4. What is the significance of Jesus' bodily resurrection?

5. If someone were to ask you, "What is grace?" what would you say?

Expand the Teaching (Optional – 30 minutes)

To expand the session to 90 minutes use one or more of the following activities. (Activity sheets for participants are located in the Participant Guide.)

- **KEY BIBLE VERSES**   This study in Scripture can be completed individually or in small groups.

- **QUICK QUIZ**   The quiz is based on the content in the DVD session, so you will want to have participants complete it only after watching the DVD.

- **READ A CREED**   Read The Apostles' Creed together as a class. (Note: The word *catholic* in the Creed means "universal".) Discuss its background and the importance of Creeds for believers.

- **PRESENTATION**   Teach through the "Christianity" section in *Christianity, Cults & Religions* PowerPoint® presentation. Also see the sections on "Seventh-day Adventism," "Unification," "Christian Science," and "Unity."

Reaching Out (5 minutes)

℘ Encourage participants to do one or both of the following activities during the coming week.

1. Choose one (or two or more!) of the key Bible verses or any of the Scripture references mentioned in this session to memorize. Memorizing Bible verses will not only be personally edifying, but will be useful to recall on-the-spot when you are in conversation with someone in a cult or another religion.

2. Read the creeds. You can find the texts of the four ecumenical (universal) creeds, as well as various denominational statements of belief, at www.creeds.net. Ask yourself, What does the creed explain about God? How can I use this teaching to discern the truth?

℘ Close the session in prayer.

Key Bible Verses

JOHN 1:1–14
"In the beginning was the Word, and the Word was with God, and the Word was God. He was with God in the beginning. Through him all things were made; without him nothing was made that has been

made. In him was life, and that life was the light of men. The light
shines in the darkness, but the darkness has not understood it. There
came a man who was sent from God; his name was John. He came
as a witness to testify concerning that light, so that through him all
men might believe. He himself was not the light; he came only as a
witness to the light. The true light that gives light to every man was
coming into the world. He was in the world, and though the world
was made through him, the world did not recognize him. He came
to that which was his own, but his own did not receive him. Yet to
all who received him, to those who believed in his name, he gave
the right to become children of God—children born not of natural
descent, nor of human decision or a husband's will, but born of God.
The Word became flesh and made his dwelling among us. We have
seen his glory, the glory of the One and Only, who came from the
Father, full of grace and truth." *NIV*

Q Jesus Christ is referred to in this passage as "the Word." What does this
passage reveal about who Jesus Christ was and is?

A **He was God since the beginning (v. 1–2). He is our savior (v. 12).
He became human (v. 14). He is the only Son of God (v. 14).**

1 CORINTHIANS 15:1–6

"Now, brothers, I want to remind you of the gospel I preached to you,
which you received and on which you have taken your stand. By
this gospel you are saved, if you hold firmly to the word I preached
to you. Otherwise, you have believed in vain. For what I received I
passed on to you as of first importance: that Christ died for our sins
according to the Scriptures, that he was buried, that he was raised
on the third day according to the Scriptures, and that he appeared
to Peter, and then to the Twelve. After that, he appeared to more
than five hundred of the brothers at the same time, most of whom
are still living, though some have fallen asleep." *NIV*

Q In your own words, what is the "gospel" that the apostle Paul is reminding
his readers of in this passage?

A **Jesus Christ died for our sins; he was buried and then resurrected
from the dead; he was seen by many eyewitnesses.**

Quick Quiz   ANSWER KEY (Answers in Bold)

1. The creeds help believers to:

    a. Recognize heresy.
    b. Distinguish essentials from nonessentials.
    c. Express the faith clearly.
    d. (a) and (b)
    e. All of the above.

2. True or False? Mary Baker Eddy, the founder of Christian Science, taught that sin, sickness, and death are unreal. **TRUE *(Christian Science denies the doctrine of human depravity and our need for God's redeeming grace.)***

3. The Bible is:

    a. Divinely inspired.
    b. Preserved by God.
    c. A collection of opinions.
    d. (a) and (b)
    e. All of the above

4. True or False? Mormonism teaches that God has always been God. **FALSE *(Mormonism affirms that our God was once a man on another world who lived, died, was resurrected, and progressed to Godhood.)***

5. The Bible teaches in Ephesians 2:8–9 that it is by __**grace**__ through faith that we are saved—and that is not from ourselves.

The Apostles' Creed

I believe in God, the Father almighty, creator of heaven and earth.

I believe in Jesus Christ, God's only Son, our Lord, who was conceived by the Holy Spirit, born of the Virgin Mary, suffered under Pontius Pilate, was crucified, died, and was buried; he descended to the dead. On the third day he rose again; he ascended into heaven, he is seated at the right hand of the Father, and he will come again to judge the living and the dead.

I believe in the Holy Spirit, the holy catholic church, the communion of saints, the forgiveness of sins, the resurrection of the body, and the life everlasting. AMEN.

Where Did the Creeds Come From?

THE APOSTLES' CREED

The apostles did not write the Apostles' Creed. No one knows for certain when this creed as written. References to and quotation of similar statements—known as the "Rule of Faith"—can be found in writings as early as the second century AD. The name "Apostles' Creed" means that the creed contains the Apostolic tradition. The Apostles' Creed is the most universal of all the creeds. Most Christian denominations continue to recite and teach it.

THE NICENE CREED

The greatest doctrinal challenge to the church arose internally. Arius, a priest in Alexandria, suggested that if God begat Jesus, then Jesus had an origin. As such, Jesus did not share in the same divine essence with the Father—making him a lesser god. This teaching became known as Arianism. In AD 325, Constantine called the leaders of the church to participate in a council—that is, an assembly of bishops. They met in the city of Nicaea, in present-day Turkey. The Council of Nicaea, made up of about 300 participants, overwhelmingly voted against the Arian teachings—ancient documents suggest that only three bishops refused to sign their agreement. The council expressed its views about God, Jesus, and the church in the Nicene Creed.

ATHANASIAN CREED

Athanasius was one of the most active opponents of Arius' teachings. His persistence and clear mind helped the church to clarify its positions and write it in a creed, the Nicene Creed. Athanasius' teachings are summarized in the Athanasian Creed. While it is likely that Athanasius did not write it, the creed contains his teachings and main ideas. The Athanasian Creed begins by affirming, "This is what the catholic [or universal] faith teaches: we worship one God in the Trinity and the Trinity in unity. We distinguish among the persons, but we do not divide the substance [or essence]." After unpacking these ideas, the creed concludes, "So that in all things, as aforesaid, the Unity in Trinity and the Trinity in Unity is to be worshipped."

DEFINITION OF CHALCEDON

Understanding the incarnation of Jesus—the embodiment of God the Son in human flesh—was one of the greatest challenges for the early church. In AD 451 the Council of Chalcedon (located in today's Turkey) provided a clear statement of the Apostolic teachings concerning Jesus. The Definition of Chalcedon made it clear that Jesus is fully God and fully human, two natures existing in perfect harmony in one person.

(Adapted from *Creeds & Heresies: Then & Now* Rose Publishing www.rose-publishing.com)

Additional Resources

Books

Know What You Believe by Paul E. Little (Victor, 2003)

Basic Christianity by John R.W. Stott (IVP, 2007)

Know the Truth: A Handbook of Christian Belief by Bruce Milne (IVP, 2010)

Conviction Without Compromise: Standing Strong in the Core Beliefs of the Christian Faith by Norman Geisler and Ron Rhodes (Harvest House, 2008)

Bible Doctrine: Essential Teachings of the Christian Faith by Wayne Grudem (Zondervan, 1999)

Creeds, Councils and Christ: Did the Early Christians Misrepresent Jesus? by Gerald Bray (Mentor, 2009)

Internet

Creeds of Christendom   www.creeds.net

Early Church   www.earlychurch.org.uk

The Gospel of Jesus Christ: An Evangelical Celebration www.apologeticsindex.org/e02.html

More from Rose Publishing

Essential Doctrine Made Easy pamphlet   (ISBN 9781596361430)

Creeds & Heresies: Then & Now pamphlet   (ISBN 9781596363489)

Why Truth Matters pamphlet   (ISBN 9781596363564)

The inclusion of a work or web site does not necessarily mean endorsement of all its contents or of other works by the same author(s) or organization.

Jehovah's Witnesses

Watchtower Bible and Tract Society

Session 3 Outline
Jehovah's Witnesses

1. Beginnings

    a. William Miller (1782–1849), Adventism

    b. Charles Taze Russell (1852–1916)

    c. Armageddon and the year 1914

    d. "Judge" Joseph Rutherford (1869–1942)

2. The Watchtower Society today

    a. Over 18 million followers

    b. *The Watchtower* and *Awake!* magazines

    c. New World Translation

    d. The 144,000; Governing Body

3. Distinctive beliefs

    a. No Trinity

        • Jesus is a lesser, created god

        • The "holy spirit" is Jehovah's invisible, active force

    b. Apostate "Christendom"

    c. "Anointed Class" and "other sheep"

    d. What is required to be saved?

        • Taking in knowledge

        • Obeying God's laws

        • Belonging to and serving in Jehovah's one true organization

- Being loyal to Jehovah's organization

e. Witnesses have to work toward perfection

f. Prohibitions

- Refusing blood transfusions

- No celebrating holidays, birthdays, etc.

- No military service, no voting, no flag salute

4. Biblical insights

a. One God

- Isaiah 43:10

- 1 Peter 1:1–2

b. The Holy Spirit is God

- 2 Corinthians 3:17

- Acts 5:3–4

c. Jesus is God

- Isaiah 9:6

- John 8:58; Exodus 3:14

- Colossians 2:9

- John 5:18, 23

- Hebrews 1:6

d. Jesus rose physically

- John 2:19

e. Salvation is a free gift

- Romans 6:23

- Acts 16:30–31

- Titus 3:5

- Philippians 3:9

5. Do's and don'ts

    a. Do remember that Jehovah's Witnesses are real people

    b. Do be courteous and respectful

    c. Do know the Bible

    d. Do ask questions

    e. Don't assume that Jehovah's Witnesses know the Bible

    f. Don't assume that there is only one right way to witness

    g. Don't try to force them to admit they're wrong

    h. Don't just turn them away

Key Terms

144,000/"anointed class"   According to Watchtower teaching, 144,000 is the number of Christians living between Pentecost (c. AD 30) and 1935, called the "anointed class" or "little flock," who will live in heaven as spirits forever. (The other class of Christians is called the "earthly class.")

Adventism   Followers of the various movements inspired by the teachings of American preacher William Miller (1782–1849) who predicted that the second coming of Christ would take place in 1843 or 1844.

Arianism   Originated in the fourth century AD and argues that Jesus doesn't share the same essence with God, and thus does not share in the same divine nature with eternity and authority. The Nicene, Chalcedonian, and Athanasian Creeds are primarily responses to this heresy.

Armageddon   According to the Watchtower, this is the final battle between wicked mankind and Jehovah God to end world governments which brings about the establishment of Jehovah's "kingdom rule" on Paradise Earth.

34

Christ's "Presence"   Watchtower teaching that the second coming of Jesus already took place invisibly in 1914.

Christendom   Disparaging term used to describe "professed Christianity"—that is, all non-Jehovah's Witness religions that claim to be Christian—in contrast with "the true Christianity of the Bible." Viewed as being under Satan's control.

Jehovah   God's personal name. Nearly all other Bibles have "LORD" for God's name in the Old Testament, but the New World Translation renders it "Jehovah"— and even "restores" the divine name to the New Testament.

New World Translation (NWT)   The official Bible of the Watchtower Society. The Watchtower has stated that other English translations have "fallen victim to the power of human traditions.... Inconsistency and unreasonableness have been insinuated into the teachings of the inspired writings." (NWT 1950)

Other Sheep   Another name Jehovah's Witnesses use for the "earthly class," drawn from John 10:16.

Theocratic Kingdom   Jehovah's kingdom rule through the Watchtower Society.

Torture Stake   The Watchtower Society teaches that Jesus was executed on an upright pole or stake instead of a two-beamed cross. Jehovah's Witnesses believe that the cross is a pagan symbol and that using it in worship violates the Second Commandment's prohibition against idolatry.

Watchtower Bible and Tract Society   The Jehovah's Witness organization, which is headquartered in Brooklyn, New York. Its "Governing Body" claims to have sole spiritual authority over Jehovah's people.

Before the Session

❦ *Prepare:*

- Ask God for guidance and pray for each participant.

- Watch DVD Session 3 on your own.

- Review *What about the 144,000?*, *Traits of God and Jesus*, and *Witnessing Tips* on the following pages.

- See *Additional Resources* for further study.

- Read *Rose Bible Basics: Christianity, Cults & Religions* handbook chapter 5.

❦ *Materials needed for this session:*

- DVD Session 3

- Bible

- New World Translation (optional)

- "Jehovah's Witnesses" section in *Christianity, Cults & Religions* PowerPoint® presentation (optional)

Opening the Session (5 minutes)

Use the *Did You Know?* facts to get participants thinking about today's topic. If you have a projector or whiteboard you can display the facts as participants enter the classroom. You can also read the facts aloud to the group before watching the DVD.

When everyone gathers together, welcome participants and open the session in prayer. If your group has new participants, you may want to briefly cover the purposes of this study (see Session 1).

Did You Know?

- The Watchtower publishes books and magazines in over 500 languages.
- The Watchtower has over 18 million followers in more than 200 countries and territories.
- Watchtower founder Charles Taze Russell predicted that the world would end in 1914, then changed the date to 1915—then again to 1918. His successor, Joseph Rutherford moved the date to 1925.
- Jehovah's Witnesses use only their own version of the Bible, the New World Translation. Its anonymous translation committee consisted of six men—five of whom had no formal training in biblical languages.

Watch the DVD   SESSION 3 (30 minutes)

- Refer class members to the session outline in their Participant Guides for note taking.

Group Discussion (20 minutes)

If the class is large, divide participants into small groups. If time allows, have a spokesperson from each small group share with the rest of the class some of the insights discussed in their group. (These questions are also located in the Participant Guide.)

1. Share about a conversation you had with a Jehovah's Witness. What things were discussed? Was it easy or difficult to discuss different beliefs?

2. What are some reasons why people become Jehovah's Witnesses?

3. What is required for someone to be "saved" according to Jehovah's Witness teaching? What is required according to the Bible?

4. What difficulties and challenges do you think someone might face if he or she left the Jehovah's Witnesses and became a Christian?

5. Do you feel ready to discuss your beliefs with Jehovah's Witnesses? Why or why not? What would help you feel ready?

Expand the Teaching (optional – 30 minutes)

To expand the session to 90 minutes use one or more of the following activities. (Activity sheets for participants are located in the Participant Guide.)

*   **KEY BIBLE VERSES**   This study in Scripture can be completed individually or in small groups.

*   **QUICK QUIZ**   The quiz is based on the content in the DVD session, so you will want to have participants complete it only after watching the DVD.

*   **PRESENTATION**   Teach through the "Jehovah's Witnesses" section in *Christianity, Cults & Religions* PowerPoint® presentation.

Reaching Out (5 minutes)

❡ Encourage participants to do one or more of the following during the week:

- Read carefully through *Witnessing Tips* in the Participant Guide.

- Reflect on these questions:

  1. What attitude do I usually have toward Jehovah's Witnesses?

  2. How have I treated Jehovah's Witnesses who have come to my door? How does God want me to treat them?

  3. What can I do to be better prepared for when Jehovah's Witnesses come knocking?

  4. Do I have a friend, coworker, or family member who is a Jehovah's Witness? If so, how can I be intentional about praying for them and looking for opportunities to tell them about the good news of the free gift of salvation?

  (These questions are also found in the Participant Guide.)

❡ Close the session in prayer.

Key Bible Verses

COLOSSIANS 2:9–10

"For in Christ all the fullness of the Deity lives in bodily form, and you have been given fullness in Christ, who is the head over every power and authority." *NIV*

Q   What do these verses tell us about who Jesus is?

A   **He is fully divine, incarnate, and rules over all powers and authorities—and that includes any earthly organization!**

ROMANS 6:23

"For the wages of sin is death, but the gift of God is eternal life in Christ Jesus our Lord." *NIV*

Q   What is eternal life as described in this verse? What does this indicate about how salvation is received?

A   **Eternal life is a gift from God—not earned; like a genuine present, it is given and simply received.**

PHILIPPIANS 3:8–9

"What is more, I consider everything a loss compared to the surpassing greatness of knowing Christ Jesus my Lord, for whose sake I have lost all things. I consider them rubbish, that I may gain Christ and be found in him, not having a righteousness of my own that comes from the law, but that which is through faith in Christ—the righteousness that comes from God and is by faith." *NIV*

Q   What does righteousness not come from? Through what does it come?

A   **Righteousness doesn't come from how well we follow religious laws, but by believing in Jesus Christ.**

Quick Quiz   Answer Key (Answers in Bold)

1. In nearly _____ places the Jehovah's Witnesses' Bible, the New World Translation, is altered to match up with Watchtower doctrines.

    a. 50
    b. 100
    c. 200
    d. 300

2. True or False? According to Watchtower teaching, only the "anointed class" of 144,000 people has the ability and the right to properly interpret the Bible. **TRUE**

3. According to Watchtower teaching, Jesus was the first thing Jehovah created, and Jesus began his existence as _____.

    a. Adam
    b. A perfect human
    c. Michael the Archangel
    d. The second Person of the Trinity
    e. None of the above

4. True or False? According to Watchtower teaching, Jehovah's Witnesses have assurance of salvation because they were baptized in Jehovah's "one true organization"—the Watchtower Society. **FALSE.** *(Jehovah's Witnesses do not have assurance of salvation –even after baptism– because they can never know if they have done enough good works to be saved.)*

5. When talking with Jehovah's Witnesses, remember to ask __**questions**__ instead of making accusations.

Witnessing Tips (Do's and Don'ts)

- *Do pray before each encounter* with the Jehovah's Witnesses and invite the Holy Spirit to lead and guide the conversation. Ask him to fill their minds and hearts with the truth of his Word.

- *Don't depend on evidence and argumentation alone.* Rely on the Holy Spirit to guide you. It's the Holy Spirit's job to convict of sin, righteousness, and judgment.

- *Do approach Jehovah's Witnesses with a humble, loving attitude.* Identify with them in genuine concern, and treat them respectfully, realizing they probably wouldn't have joined had they known all the facts.

- *Don't approach them with a superior attitude,* belittle them, or act like you have something they don't.

- *Do ask the Jehovah's Witness to help you understand how to reconcile their beliefs with the Bible.* Jehovah's Witnesses are trained to teach, not to listen to you. Questions can be a powerful tool to break through their programmed responses and to get them to "think" for themselves.

- *Don't confront Jehovah's Witnesses in an argumentative manner,* trying to "teach" them. Jehovah's Witnesses believe they have "the Truth" and that you don't have anything to offer them.

- *Do challenge the Jehovah's Witnesses' trust in the Watchtower* by showing discrepancies in their own literature. Jehovah's Witnesses are not allowed to read anti-Watchtower literature, so use their literature and Scripture alone.

- *Don't engage in deep scriptural discussion too soon.* Witnesses are told they can't understand the Bible apart from Watchtower literature, so their trust in the Watchtower needs to be broken before they can begin to interpret the Bible for themselves.

- *Do pray to "Jehovah God" with Jehovah's Witnesses* and pray about personal things that are happening in their lives. Emphasize the "Father" aspect of "Jehovah" in your prayer and how he cares for you personally.

- *Don't pray to "God" or "Lord" without addressing the prayer to "Jehovah" at some point.* Jehovah's Witnesses fear that if a prayer doesn't have Jehovah's name, it may end up in Satan's hands. Also, don't ask if you can pray with them for healing of sickness (unless they approach you privately). They're taught that God doesn't "heal" today, and anything miraculous is done by Satan to deceive the unsuspecting.

- *Do tell Jehovah's Witnesses about your personal relationship with Jesus* and how he answers prayer and personally works in your life. Jehovah's Witnesses do not believe God cares as much for them as he does for the organization, so your testimony can make them hungry for a real relationship with the true God.

- *Don't try to force the Jehovah's Witness to "agree" with you.* They're not allowed to disagree with the Watchtower, so plant seeds of doubt through your questions and let the Holy Spirit do his work.

- *Do be available, persistent, and patient.* If they're asking questions, they're starting to think for themselves. This is the first step in leaving the Watchtower.

(Excerpt from *10 Q&A on Jehovah's Witnesses* Rose Publishing www.rose-publishing.com)

What about the 144,000?

According to the Watchtower Society, there are two very different classes of Christians. One is a special group of 144,000 people known as the "anointed class" (also called the "heavenly class," "little flock," or "faithful and discreet slave"). They lived between Pentecost (c. AD 30) and 1935, and will one day live in heaven as spirits forever. Only members of this special class...

- are part of the new covenant and have Jesus as their mediator.

- are "born again" and have "adoption" as God's children.

- are true members of the "Christian congregation," the church.

- may partake of the "memorial emblems" of Jesus' Last Supper (Communion) once a year.

- spiritually guide God's organization today and will rule from heaven over the earth.

There is also a much larger group, the "earthly class" (also called the "other sheep" or "great crowd"). This includes virtually everyone who has become a Jehovah's Witness after 1935, along with people throughout time who weren't wicked but never heard of Christ. They will have a chance to live forever as human beings in a paradise on earth.

The heavenly and earthly classes will remain eternally separated. The earthly class will never see the Father or Jesus.

But according to the Bible, there is no "two-class" system. Christ is the mediator between God and all people who are redeemed in him (1 Timothy 2:5–6). Everyone who has faith in Christ is already "born again" (1 Peter 1:3; 1 John 5:1). Everyone who knows God as Father through Jesus Christ has the "adoption as sons" (Romans 8:14–17; Galatians 4:4–6) and is his child (John 1:12–13). All baptized believers are part of the church, the body of Christ (1 Corinthians 12:13).

All true believers will live together in the new heaven and new earth. Scripture teaches that when believers in Christ die, they go immediately into God's presence (Luke 23:43; Philippians 1:21–24). All believers from all ages will be resurrected with immortal bodies like Christ's (Romans 8:11; 1 Corinthians 15:42–54; Philippians 3:21) and live together in the new heaven and new earth

(Matthew 5:5; 2 Peter 3:13; Revelation 21:1). Believers in Christ will "reign on the earth" (Revelation 5:10). (Note: This "reign" may refer to God's intention for people to exercise dominion on earth [Genesis 1:26, 28] or to Christians ruling over the redeemed from past ages.) All of the redeemed will see the Father and Jesus (Matthew 5:8; 1 John 3:2; Revelation 21:3–4).

So, who are the 144,000? The Bible only refers to "144,000" in Revelation chapters 7 and 14. Christians who interpret the number literally also take the twelve Israelite tribes of 12,000 literally (Revelation 7:4–8). It makes no sense to take the number 144,000 literally but not the twelve groups of 12,000 that the text adds up to get 144,000. Christians who take the twelve tribes in this passage as symbolizing the church consistently regard the number 144,000 as symbolic. But there is no basis in Revelation 7—or any other Bible passage—for dividing Jesus' followers into two classes.

(Adapted from *10 Q&A on Jehovah's Witnesses* Rose Publishing www.rose-publishing.com)

Traits of God and Jesus

The Watchtower teaches that Jesus is a lesser god than Jehovah. However, Scripture portrays Jesus as co-equal with God the Father, demonstrating Jesus' deity.

Traits Unique to God (Jehovah)	Traits of Jesus
Creation is "the work of his hands"—alone (Gen. 1:1; Ps. 102:25; Isa. 44:24)	Creation is "the work of his hands"—all things created in and through him (John 1:3; Col. 1:16; Heb. 1:2, 10)
"The first and the last" (Isa. 44:6)	"The first and the last" (Rev. 1:17; 22:13)
"Lord of lords" (Deut. 10:17; Ps. 136:3)	"Lord of lords" (1 Tim. 6:15; Rev. 17:14; 19:16)
Unchanging and eternal (Ps. 90:2; 102:26–27; Mal. 3:6)	Unchanging and eternal (John 8:58; Col. 1:17; Heb. 1:11–12; 13:8)
Judge of all people (Gen. 18:25; Ps. 94:2; 96:13; 98:9)	Judge of all people (John 5:22; Acts 17:31; 2 Cor. 5:10; 2 Tim. 4:1)
Only Savior; no other God can save (Isa. 43:11; 45:21–22; Hos. 13:4)	Savior of the world; no salvation apart from him (John 4:42; Acts 4:12; Titus 2:13; 1 John 4:14)
Redeems from their sins a people for his own possession (Ex. 19:5; Ps. 130:7–8; Ezek. 37:23)	Redeems from their sins a people for his own possession (Titus 2:14)
Hears and answers prayers of those who call on him (Ps. 86:5–8; Isa. 55:6–7; Jer. 33:3; Joel 2:32)	Hears and answers prayers of those who call on him (John 14:14; Rom. 10:12–13; 1 Cor. 1:2; 2 Cor. 12:8–9)
Only God has divine glory (Isa. 42:8; 48:11)	Jesus has divine glory (John 17:5)
Worshiped by angels (Ps. 97:7)	Worshiped by angels (Heb. 1:6)

Additional Resources

❦ Books

Jehovah's Witnesses by Robert M. Bowman, Jr. (Zondervan, 1995)

Reasoning from the Scriptures with the Jehovah's Witnesses by Ron Rhodes (Harvest House, 1993)

How to Rescue Your Loved One from the Watchtower by David A. Reed (Baker, 1989)

Why You Should Believe in the Trinity: An Answer to Jehovah's Witnesses by Robert M. Bowman, Jr. (Baker, 1989)

What Does God Require? Biblical Answers to Questions Jehovah's Witnesses Ask by Christy (Harvey) Darlington (Witnesses for Jesus, 2001)

Jehovah's Witnesses: Their Claims, Doctrinal Changes, and Prophetic Speculation. What Does the Record Show? by Edmund C. Gruss (Xulon, 2001)

Pilgrimage Through the Watchtower by Kevin Quick (Baker, 1989)

Crisis of Conscience by Raymond Franz (Commentary, 1999)

❦ Internet

Witnesses for Jesus   www.4jehovah.org

Free Minds   www.freeminds.org

Facts About Jehovah's Witnesses   www.jwfacts.com

TowerWatch Ministries   www.towerwatch.com.

❦ DVD

In the Name of Jehovah (NAMB, 2004).

The Witness at Your Door and *The Witness Goes Out* (Jeremiah Films, 1992)

Witnesses of Jehovah (Good News Defenders, 1988)

❦ More From Rose Publishing

10 Questions & Answers on Jehovah's Witnesses PowerPoint® (ISBN 9781596361225)

The Trinity pamphlet (ISBN 9781890947026)

The inclusion of a work or web site does not necessarily mean endorsement of all its contents or of other works by the same author(s) or organization.

Mormonism

The Church of Jesus Christ of Latter-day Saints

Session 4 Outline
Mormonism

1. Early Mormonism

    a. Joseph Smith, Jr. (1805–1844)

    - First Vision (Sacred Grove)

    - Visitations by Moroni

    - Moving to Ohio, Missouri, and Illinois

    - Assassination

    b. Brigham Young (1801–1877)

2. On what do Mormons base their beliefs?

    a. Four "standard works"

    - The Bible—King James Version

    - Book of Mormon

    - Doctrine and Covenants

    - Pearl of Great Price (Includes the Book of Abraham)

    b. Living prophets

3. Mormon teachings

    a. God is not a Trinity

    b. "Holy Ghost" (a personage); "holy spirit" (a fluid-like substance)

    c. Jesus, "elder brother" and firstborn spirit child

    d. Adam fell "up"; No sin nature

    e. Afterlife

    - Three "degrees of glory" (Telestial, Terrestrial, Celestial)

    - Outer darkness

4. Mormon practices

   a. "Word of Wisdom": no caffeine drinks, alcohol, tobacco

   b. Temple rituals: endowments

   c. Individual blood atonement

5. What is the appeal of Mormonism?

   a. Family emphasis

   b. Social activities

   c. Baptism on behalf of deceased relatives

6. What does the Bible say?

   a. "even if an angel..."

      • Galatians 1:6–8

   b. No gods before or after God

      • Isaiah 43:10; 40–45

   c. God is not a man

      • Numbers 23:19; Hosea 11:9; Romans 1:22–23

   d. Jesus Christ has always been God

      • John 1:1

      • Matthew 1; Luke 1

   e. The gospel of salvation

      • Romans 3:20–23; 6:23

      • Ephesians 2:8–10

   f. Jesus preserves his church

      • Matthew 16:18

   g. Testing prophets

      • 1 John 4:1

- Deuteronomy 13:1–5; 18:21–22

7. Mormon missionaries at your door

   a. Don't question their motives

   b. Don't ridicule their beliefs

   c. Don't let them pray for you

   d. Don't agree to pray about the Book of Mormon; instead, test by Scripture

      - Acts 17:11

   e. Take them through the Scriptures

   f. Tell them what Jesus has done for you

      - 1 John 5:10–13

   g. End on a positive note

Key Terms

Book of Abraham   Mormon scripture, now published as part of the Pearl of Great Price. In 1835 Joseph Smith purchased Egyptian artifacts from a traveling showman, announcing that they contained the writings of the biblical patriarch Abraham. The "translation" he produced, called the Book of Abraham, was debunked when papyri from the collection were rediscovered in 1967.

Book of Mormon   Mormon scripture said to have been translated by Joseph Smith from gold plates he received from the angel Moroni in 1827. It purports to tell the story of three people groups (the Lehites, Jaredites, and Mulekites) that migrated from the Middle East to the Americas, roughly between 2000 BC and AD 400. After being translated, the plates were taken back to heaven.

Celestial Kingdom   The highest of three heavenly "degrees of glory" awaiting faithful Latter-day Saints. Entrance into this kingdom is gained by complete obedience to the Mormon gospel, and those who reach its highest level become gods.

Doctrine and Covenants   Mormon scripture containing modern revelations, most given by Joseph Smith.

Endowment Ceremony   Secret temple ritual performed by living persons, sometimes on behalf of the dead. Required for exaltation.

Eternal Progression   Human progression starting from a pre-existent spirit, then into a human body, and then finally on to godhood.

Exaltation   Synonymous with eternal life. Only Mormons who gain exaltation have the ability to become gods and procreate throughout eternity.

Freemasonry (Masonic Lodge)   A secret society founded in London in the early 18th century. Known for its use of symbolism and secret rituals. Elements of Freemasonry are found in the Mormon temple endowment ceremony.

Inspired Version   Also known as the Joseph Smith Translation, this adaptation of the Bible was completed by Joseph Smith in 1833.

Lamanites and Nephites   According to the Book of Mormon, followers of Nephi and Laman, the sons of the Prophet Lehi who led his family to the New World prior to the capture of Jerusalem (c. 600 BC). Those who followed the wicked Laman were shown God's displeasure by being cursed with a dark skin (2 Nephi 5:21–25); they are considered the ancestors of the American Indians and Polynesians.

Moroni   Ancient Nephite leader who buried the gold plates containing the Book of Mormon and later appeared as an angel to Joseph Smith to tell him of their location. His image is found on many LDS temples throughout the world.

Pearl of Great Price   Mormon scripture containing the Book of Abraham, Book of Moses, and other short works.

Polygamy   Between 1852 and 1890 the practice of plural marriage became essential for any Mormon man hoping to achieve exaltation. The Mormon Church's sixth president had five wives and fathered 43 children. The Mormon Church renounced polygamy in 1890, and Utah was then granted statehood when anti-polygamy laws were written into the state constitution.

Priesthood   The basis on which Mormon males have power and authority to act on behalf of God. It consists of two orders: the Aaronic (or lesser) priesthood, and the Melchizedek priesthood. Males of African descent were denied the Mormon priesthood until 1978.

Telestial Kingdom   The lowest of three heavenly "degrees of glory" to which the worst sinners are sent to after death. The Holy Ghost will visit people in this kingdom, but the Father and Son will not.

Temples   Special buildings reserved for ordinances for the dead (including baptism for the dead), marriages for "time and eternity," and "sealings" of families for eternity.

Terrestrial Kingdom   The middle of three heavenly "degrees of glory," to which good people who are not Mormons are sent to after death. Jesus will visit people in this heaven, but God the Father will not.

Urim and Thummim   A translation device described by Joseph Smith as "two stones in silver bows." Allegedly received from Moroni together with the gold plates containing the text of the Book of Mormon. (Said to be the same as the Urim and Thummim mentioned in such biblical passages as Exodus 28:30.)

Word of Wisdom   Section 89 in Doctrine and Covenants which prohibits the consumption of caffeine drinks, alcohol, and tobacco.

Session 4

Before the Session

❧ *Prepare:*

- Ask God for guidance and pray for each participant.

- Watch DVD Session 4 on your own.

- Review *Joseph Smith: Prophet or Fraud?* and *Witnessing Tips* on the following pages.

- See *Additional Resources* for further study.

- Read *Rose Bible Basics: Christianity, Cults & Religions* handbook chapter 6.

❧ *Materials needed for this session:*

- DVD Session 4

- Bible

- Book of Mormon (optional)

- "Mormonism" section in *Christianity, Cults & Religions* PowerPoint® presentation (optional)

Opening the Session (5 minutes)

Use the *Did You Know?* facts to get participants thinking about today's topic. If you have a projector or whiteboard you can display the facts as participants enter the classroom. You can also read the facts aloud to the group before watching the DVD.

When everyone gathers together, welcome participants and open the session in prayer. If your group has new participants, you may want to briefly cover the purposes of this study (see Session 1).

Did You Know?

- The Mormon Church has over 13 million members in more than 160 countries, and over 50,000 full-time missionaries. The Mormon Church produces materials in over 160 languages.
- The fifth Mormon prophet declared: "As man is, God once was; as God is, man may become." *(Teachings of Lorenzo Snow, p. 1)*
- Brigham Young said, "The only men who become Gods, even the Sons of God, are those who enter into polygamy." *(Journal of Discourses, vol. 11, p. 269)*
- Mormonism teaches that God resides near the planet Kolob with one or more wives.

Watch the DVD   SESSION 4 (35 minutes)

- Refer class members to the session outline in their Participant Guides for note taking.

Group Discussion (15 minutes)

If the class is large, divide participants into small groups. If time allows, have a spokesperson from each small group share with the rest of the class some of the insights discussed in their group. (These questions are also located in the Participant Guide.)

1. Share about a conversation you had with a Mormon. What things were discussed? Was it easy or difficult to discuss different beliefs?

2. What are some reasons why people join the Mormon Church?

3. What was the purpose of Jesus' death and resurrection according to Mormonism? What was the purpose according to the Bible?

4. What difficulties and challenges do you think someone might face if he or she left the Mormon Church and became a Christian?

5. Do you feel ready to discuss your beliefs with Mormons? Why or why not? What would help you feel ready?

Expand the Teaching (optional – 30 minutes)

To expand the session to 90 minutes use one or more of the following activities. (Activity sheets for participants are located in the Participant Guide.)

*   **KEY BIBLE VERSES**   This study in Scripture can be completed individually or in small groups.

*   **QUICK QUIZ**   The quiz is based on the content in the DVD session, so you will want to have participants complete it only after watching the DVD.

*   **PRESENTATION**   Teach through the "Mormonism" section in *Christianity, Cults & Religions* PowerPoint® presentation.

Reaching Out (5 minutes)

₢ *Encourage participants to do one or more of the following during the week:*

*   Read carefully through *Witnessing Tips* in the Participant Guide.

*   Reflect on these questions:

    1. What attitude do I usually have toward Mormons? How have I treated Mormons whom I've known? How does God want me to treat them?

    2. What can I do to be better prepared for when Mormon missionaries come knocking?

    3. Do I have a friend, coworker, or family member who is a Mormon? If so, how can I be intentional about praying for them and looking for opportunities to tell them my testimony of what God has done in my life?

₢ *Close the session in prayer.*

Key Bible Verses

GALATIANS 1:6–8

"I am astonished that you are so quickly deserting the one who called you by the grace of Christ and are turning to a different gospel—which is really no gospel at all. Evidently some people are throwing you into confusion and are trying to pervert the gospel of Christ. But even if we or an angel from heaven should preach a gospel other than the one we preached to you, let him be eternally condemned!" *NIV*

Q   Why is belief in a "different gospel" so dangerous?

A   **It's a desertion of Jesus, a perversion of the truth, and gospel that cannot save.**

MATTHEW 16:16–18

"Simon Peter answered, 'You are the Christ, the Son of the living God.' Jesus replied, 'Blessed are you, Simon son of Jonah, for this was not revealed to you by man, but by my Father in heaven. And I tell you that you are Peter, and on this rock I will build my church, and the gates of Hades will not overcome it.'" *NIV*

Q   What does Jesus promise about his church?

A   **Jesus will build his church, and it will never be destroyed.**

ROMANS 3:20–22

"By the works of the Law no flesh will be justified in His sight; for through the Law comes the knowledge of sin. But now apart from the Law the righteousness of God has been manifested, being witnessed by the Law and the Prophets, even the righteousness of God through faith in Jesus Christ for all those who believe; for there is no distinction; for all have sinned and fall short of the glory of God." *NASB*

Q   How are believers made righteous?

A   **By faith in Jesus, not by observance of the Law. The Law only makes us aware of our sinfulness.**

Quick Quiz   ANSWER KEY (Answers in Bold)

1. Which of the following is *not* true about Joseph Smith, the founder of the Mormon Church?

   a. He claimed God commissioned him to restore the church on earth.
   b. He ran for president of the United States.
   c. He claimed that John the Baptist appeared to him.
   d. **He was thrown in jail because he refused to stop preaching forgiveness. (Smith was actually jailed for money-digging and again later for ordering the destruction of a newspaper's printing press when it denounced his polygamy.)**
   e. He "married" some of the wives of his colleagues.

2. True or False? The Mormon Church claims that the Book of Mormon is an historical record of ancient Hebraic peoples who came from the Middle East to the Americas. **TRUE (Although the Mormon church makes this claim, there is no archaeological evidence—nor a single city mentioned in the Book of Mormon—which can be found to support this claim.)**

3. According to Mormon teaching, Jesus was the eldest of God's spirit children and __**Lucifer**__ was his younger, jealous brother. **(Lucifer was jealous that Jesus was chosen to be the Savior instead of him, so after Lucifer led an unsuccessful rebellion among the heavenly beings he was cast down to earth and became the Devil.)**

4. According to the Bible, which of the following is true about salvation?

   a. Salvation cannot be earned by personal worthiness.
   b. Good works are the result of salvation, not its basis.
   c. Salvation is maintained by full obedience to the law.
   d. **(a) and (b) (See Romans 3:20–23)**
   e. All of the above

5. In Acts 17:11, the Berean Christians searched the __**Scriptures**__ to test whether the Apostle Paul's message was from God.

Witnessing Tips (Do's and Don'ts)

- *Don't assume* that a Mormon defines a word in the same way you do.

- *Do define your terms*—and have them define theirs. (For example, "What do you believe about salvation? About eternal life? Are they the same, or different?")

- *Don't assume what an individual Mormon believes.* Not all Mormons agree with their leaders. This could be because they are not aware of what their leaders have taught. For example, if a Mormon appears to answer a question biblically, you may respond by saying something like, "That is exactly what the Bible teaches; however, are you aware that prophet so-and-so said just the opposite? Shouldn't they be in harmony with the Bible if they are getting their information from the same God who gave us the Bible?"

- *Do ask Mormons what they believe.* Rather than accusing, ask a question.

- *Don't dwell on topics that are especially sensitive to Mormons* and should only be addressed after they feel more comfortable discussing religious issues with you. Talking about the temple ceremony, the sacred garments, polygamy, or racism will almost certainly bring the discussion to a close. Use your time wisely.

- *Do concentrate on core issues.* What the Mormon believes about God the Father, Jesus Christ, and the Holy Spirit, as well as the issue of salvation, should be primary. Do your Mormon acquaintances have the assurance that when they die all of their sins are forgiven? Do they feel confident they will receive the best their religion has to offer (godhood, eternal increase)? If so, how so? If not, why not?

- *Don't be surprised if Mormons are suspicious of Christian literature.* Mormons often feel that information written about their church, but not by their church, is almost always inaccurate. If you do use Christian material, makes sure it is well-documented. Rather than insisting that the material is correct, have Mormons show you where the information could be wrong. To do this they will need to read the material and check the references.

- *Do memorize certain points and quotes.* This often works better than using printed material because it shows the Mormon that you have taken the time to read LDS resources. Quote directly from LDS sources if possible. Statements from LDS leaders work best.

- *Don't think you need to cover every topic in one sitting.* Sometimes dealing with one or two subjects makes it easier to remember what you talked about.

- *Do be patient.* Mormons are led to believe that leaving the LDS church will lead to damnation. This is not a decision most Mormons make in an instant.

(Excerpt from *10 Q&A on Mormonism* Rose Publishing www.rose-publishing.com.)

Joseph Smith: Prophet or Fraud?

"Joseph Smith, the Prophet and Seer of the Lord, has done more, save Jesus only, for the salvation of men in this world, than any other man that ever lived in it." —*Doctrine and Covenants* 135:3

Joseph Smith denounced the Trinity:

"Many men say there is one God; the Father, the Son and the Holy Ghost are only one God! I say that is a strange God anyhow—three in one, and one in three! It is a curious organization. All are to be crammed into one God, according to sectarianism. It would make the biggest God in all the world. He would be a wonderfully big God—he would be a giant or a monster."—*Teachings of the Prophet Joseph Smith*, p. 372

Joseph Smith boasted that he accomplished more than the apostles or Jesus:

"I have more to boast of than ever any man had. I am the only man that has ever been able to keep a whole church together since the days of Adam. A large majority of the whole have stood by me. Neither Paul, John, Peter, nor Jesus ever did it. I boast that no man ever did such a work as I. The followers of Jesus ran away from Him; but the Latter-day Saints never ran away from me yet."—*History of the Church*, Vol. 6, pp. 408–412

Mormonism stands or falls on Joseph Smith:

"Mormonism, as it is called, *must stand or fall on the story of Joseph Smith.* He was either a prophet of God, divinely called, properly appointed and commissioned, or he was one of the biggest frauds this world has ever seen. *There is no middle ground.*"—Mormon prophet Joseph Fielding Smith, *Doctrines of Salvation*, Vol. 1, p. 188 (italics in original)

No salvation without Joseph Smith:

> "If it had not been for Joseph Smith and the restoration, there would be no salvation."—Mormon apostle Bruce R. McConkie, *Mormon Doctrine* (1978), p. 670

> "I know that Joseph Smith is a Prophet of God, that this is the Gospel of salvation, and if you do not believe it you will be damned, every one of you."—Mormon prophet Brigham Young, *Journal of Discourses*, Vol. 4, p. 298

> "… no man or woman in this dispensation will ever enter into the celestial kingdom of God without the consent of Joseph Smith."—Brigham Young, *Journal of Discourses*, Vol. 7, p. 289

Additional Resources

ℂ *Books*

Speaking the Truth in Love to Mormons by Mark Cares (WELS, 1998)

Mormonism 101: Examining the Religion of the Latter-day Saints by Bill McKeever and Eric Johnson (Baker, 2000)

Answering Mormons' Questions by Bill McKeever (Bethany, 1991)

By His Own Hand Upon Papyrus: A New Look at the Joseph Smith Papyri by Charles M. Larson (IRR, 1992)

What Every Mormon (and Non-Mormon) Should Know by Edmund Gruss and Lane Thuet (Xulon, 2006)

Out of Mormonism: A Woman's True Story by Judy Robertson (Bethany, 2001)

ℂ *Internet*

Living Hope Ministries   www.lhvm.org

Mormonism Research Ministry   www.mrm.org

Mormons in Transition   www.irr.org/mit

Utah Lighthouse Ministry   www.utlm.org

ℂ *DVD*

The Mormon Puzzle   (NAMB, 2004)

The Bible vs. the Book of Mormon   (Living Hope, 2005)

The Bible vs. Joseph Smith   (Living Hope, 2010)

The Lost Book of Abraham   (IRR, 2002)

ℂ *More from Rose Publishing*

10 Questions & Answers on Mormonism PowerPoint®   (ISBN 9781596361195)

The inclusion of a work or web site does not necessarily mean endorsement of all its contents or of other works by the same author(s) or organization.

Eastern Spirituality

Hinduism, Buddhism, and the New Age

Session 5 Outline
Eastern Spirituality

1. Eastern religions' arrival and impact in North America

   a. Swami Vivekananda—1893

   b. Paramahansa Yogananda—1920

   c. Oriental Exclusion Act—ended 1965

   d. New Age Movement—1980s

2. Three common threads

   a. Pantheism

   b. Reincarnation, karma

   c. Yoga, meditation

3. Hinduism

   a. Hindu scriptures (Four Vedas, Upanishads, Bhagavad Gita)

   b. Polytheism; Brahman-Atman

   c. Salvation in Hinduism

   d. Three major expressions

   • Vaishnavism

   • Shaivism

   • Shaktism

4. Buddhism

   a. Siddhartha Gautama

   b. No God is needed

   c. Four Noble Truths

   • Suffering

- Ignorance

- Nirvana

- Eightfold Path

   d.   Three major expressions

- Theravada ("path of the elders")

- Mahayana ("greater vehicle")

- Vajrayana ("diamond vehicle")

5.   New Age Movement

   a.   Transcendentalism, spiritualism, Theosophy

   b.   Rejection of traditional Christianity

   c.   What is the attraction?

- Personal godhood

- Freedom to explore

- Rejecting traditional religious approaches

- Techniques for enlightenment

- Physical healing

- Planetary transformation

6.   How do we apply the Bible?

   a.   The one true God is personal and distinct from his creation

- Genesis 1; Romans 1

   b.   Jesus is the unique redeemer

- 1 Timothy 2:15; Matthew 7:13; John 14:6

   c.   Reincarnation undermines justice

- Hebrews 9:27

   d.   Resurrection, not reincarnation

- John 5:28

- John 6:40

- Philippians 3:10

e. Christian meditation is about attachment to God

- Psalm 48:9

Key Terms

Bhagavad Gita   (c. AD 100) One of the best-known sacred writings of Hinduism, an epic poem whose central figure is the deity Krishna.

Bodhisattva   ("enlightened existence," "awakened being") One who aspires to buddhahood but postpones his own enlightenment to alleviate the suffering of others by his own merits.

Brahman-Atman   In Hinduism, Brahman is the Divine Totality, the ultimate reality, and Atman is the individual soul, like a spark from the huge fire of Brahman. God is not a personal creator, distinct from his creation, but both the creature and its source are part of the same "big reality," called Brahman-Atman.

Enlightenment   ("awakening") The realization that souls have the illusion of being reincarnated and floating through eternity bound in ignorance and suffering senselessly in one body after another.

Four Vedas   ("knowledge") The earliest Hindu texts, written approximately 1500–1000 BC.

Guru   ("teacher") The highest rank of spiritual teacher in Hinduism, Jainism and Sikhism. One who has attained enlightenment or salvation after thousands of reincarnations.

Hare Krishna   The International Society for Krishna Consciousness (ISKCON), founded in New York in 1966 by Swami Prabhubada (1896–1977). Vaishnava sect whose followers became known for their saffron robes, dancing on city streets, and aggressive fundraising techniques.

Hindu Countermission   A response by Hindus to Christian missionary efforts in which gurus are sent abroad to convert Westerners.

Karma   ("act") The spiritual principle of cause and effect, in which some kind of reward or punishment follows one's every act, whether good or bad. Thus, in Hinduism a person's past actions govern his present life, and future lives (reincarnations) are determined by past and present actions.

Mahayana   ("greater vehicle") Branch of Buddhism emphasizing that all may attain the essential Buddha-nature through meditation and the aid of bodhisattvas.

Maya   Illusion, unreality, dream. The power that causes people to believe in the false idea of duality or the phenomenal (material) world.

Moksha   ("liberation") Release or salvation in Hinduism.

Nirvana   ("extinction") The final liberation in Buddhism. Literally means "blowing out," like a candle flame. The end of all personal existence.

Noble Eightfold Path   In Buddhism, this is the means by which one pursues release from transcience and suffering, with nirvana as the ultimate goal. Consists of right understanding, thoughts, speech, actions, livelihood, endeavor, mindfulness, and concentration.

Oriental Exclusion Act   (1924) Severely restricted immigration from Asia to the United States. After it ended in 1965, many representatives of eastern religions began proselytizing in the U.S.

Pantheism   (Greek *pan*, "all," and *theos*, "God") The teaching that God is not separate from his creation, but a vague impersonal force.

Paramahansa Yogananda   (1893–1952) Founded the Self-Realization Fellowship in 1920. Most famous for his book *Autobiography of a Yogi* (1946).

Polytheism   (*poly* "many," *theos* "God) The belief in many gods. This is the most common form of ancient religion found worldwide, and still exists today in many forms.

Reincarnation   Each soul is reborn literally thousands of times before achieving liberation, or salvation. (Also called transmigration or metempsychosis.)

Samsara   ("flow together") The wandering that is the fate of the soul over many reincarnations.

Shaivism   A Hindu tradition with multiple expressions. The most significant, Shaiva Siddhanta, is theistic rather than impersonalistic.

Shaktism   A Hindu tradition emphasizing devotion to Shakti or the Devi (the divine mother) as the ultimate expression of the godhead.

Swami Vivekananda   (1863–1902) Indian devotee of Ramakrishna who famously introduced Hinduism to many Americans through his appearance at the World's Parliament of Religions in 1893.

Tantrism   A philosophy in Hinduism and Buddhism which emphasizes union of male and female principles through a variety of ritual techniques, including sexual intercourse.

Theravada   ("path of the elders") Branch of Buddhism emphasizing Samadhi ("concentration") meditation and Vipassana ("insight") meditation. Strongly affirms the existence of the historical Buddha ("Sakyamuni").

Transcendental Meditation (TM)   Maharishi Mahesh Yogi (1917–2008) founded the TM movement in India in 1957 (as the Spiritual Regeneration Movement). TM emphasizes a "mechanical" path to enlightenment. Gained early popularity through the Yogi's association with the Beatles, the Beach Boys, and other entertainers in the 1960s.

Upanishads   Over 100 Hindu philosophical treatises written approximately 800–500 BC.

Vaishnavism   A Hindu tradition that emphasizes the worship of Vishnu. Understands Brahman in terms of more personal manifestations (such as Ram and Krishna, hero of the Bhagavad Gita).

Vajrayana   ("diamond vehicle") Branch of Buddhism made popular in the West by the Dalai Lama. Combines Mahayana, Indian Tantra, and the occultic Bön religion of ancient Tibet (which promotes the worship of dark spirits). Shingon Buddhism in Japan is derived from Vajrayana.

Yoga and Meditation   Physical and mental practices developed as ways of reducing one's karma—the attachment to the physical world and our individual selves.

Zen Buddhism   Imported from China and established as a separate school in Japan in the 12th century. Emphasizes sudden and spontaneous enlightenment—the experience of one's true nature.

Before the Session

ℭ *Prepare:*

- Ask God for guidance and pray for each participant.

- Watch DVD Session 5 on your own.

- Review *The Dali Lama* and *Witnessing Tips* on the following pages.

- See *Additional Resources* for further study.

- Read *Rose Bible Basics: Christianity, Cults & Religions* handbook chapter 3.

ℭ *Materials needed for this session:*

- DVD Session 5

- Bible

- "Hinduism," "Buddhism" and "New Age" sections in *Christianity, Cults & Religions* PowerPoint® presentation (optional)

Opening the Session (5 minutes)

Use the *Did You Know?* facts to get participants thinking about today's topic. If you have a projector or whiteboard you can display the facts as participants enter the classroom. You can also read the facts aloud to the group before watching the DVD.

When everyone gathers together, welcome participants and open the session in prayer. If your group has new participants, you may want to briefly cover the purposes of this study (see Session 1).

Did You Know?

- In 1900 an estimated 1% of Americans believed in reincarnation. Today, it's roughly 25%.
- In 2009, one-quarter of U.S. adults expressed belief in one or more Eastern or New Age religious ideas, including yoga as "a spiritual practice" and "spiritual energy located in physical things" such as crystals.
- As of 2007, Buddhism was the fourth-largest belief group in the United States.
- In Hinduism there are said to be as many as 33 million gods.

Watch the DVD   SESSION 5 (30 minutes)

- Refer class members to the session outline in their Participant Guides for note taking.

Group Discussion (20 minutes)

If the class is large, divide participants into small groups. If time allows, have a spokesperson from each small group share with the rest of the class some of the insights discussed in their group. (These questions are also located in the Participant Guide.)

1. After watching this session, what did you learn about eastern spirituality that you didn't know or misunderstood before?

2. Share about a time when you had an interaction or conversation with someone in an eastern religion. What did you learn from that experience?

3. How would you describe Jesus of Christianity to someone who believes Jesus was a guru or an enlightened person (bodhisattva)?

4. How would you respond to someone who says this? "Eastern religions and Christianity are basically the same. They're just different paths to escaping pain and getting to God."

5. What difficulties and challenges do you think someone who is a follower of an eastern religion would face if he or she became a Christian?

Expand the Teaching (optional – 30 minutes)

To expand the session to 90 minutes use one or more of the following activities. (Activity sheets for participants are located in the Participant Guide.)

- **Key Bible Verses** This study in Scripture can be completed individually or in small groups.

- **Quick Quiz** The quiz is based on the content in the DVD session, so you will want to have participants complete it only after watching the DVD.

- **Presentation** Teach through the "Buddhism," "Hinduism" and "New Age" sections in *Christianity, Cults & Religions* PowerPoint® presentation. Also see sections on "Hare Krishna," " TM," "Sikhism," and "Soka Gakkai."

Reaching Out (5 minutes)

℘ Encourage participants to do one or more of the following during the week:

- Read carefully through *Witnessing Tips* in the Participant Guide.

- Reflect on these questions:

  1. Is my meditation about moving closer to God, or is it about detachment from life?

  2. Do I know the Bible well enough to show someone the uniqueness of the life and claims of Jesus Christ?

  3. Pray for someone you know who is involved in an eastern religion or the New Age. When and how do you think God might be leading you to share the gospel with this person?

- From your research in preparing for this session locate and print out or photocopy a testimony of someone who came to Christ out of an eastern religion (see www.karma2grace.org for testimonies). Give each participant a copy to take home and read during the week.

℘ Close the session in prayer.

Key Bible Verses

HEBREWS 9:27

"...it is appointed unto men once to die, but after this the judgment."
KJV

Q What does this verse reveal about the afterlife?

A **It is not an endless cycle of rebirth on earth. God has chosen to give us one life on earth before being brought to account.**

JOHN 14:6

"Jesus answered, 'I am the way and the truth and the life. No one comes to the Father except through me.'" *NIV*

Q How many ways are there to God? What—or who—is the way to God?

A **One way. It is only through Jesus that we can be reconciled to God the Father.**

PSALM 48:9

"Within your temple, O God, we meditate on your unfailing love."
NIV

PSALM 1:2

"But his delight is in the law of the LORD, and on his law he meditates day and night." *NIV*

Q What is the focus of Christian meditation?

A **God's law and his love. It is God-focused, not self-focused.**

Quick Quiz   ANSWER KEY (Answers in Bold)

1. At the root of much of today's "spirituality" is _____,
   an ancient religion.

   a. Buddhism
   b. Hinduism
   c. Theravada
   d. Astrology

2. True or False? In Buddhism, there is a creator behind the reality of the
   cosmos that explains it. **FALSE (In Buddhism, God is not needed.
   The Buddha taught that the pursuit of God is irrelevant and can
   hinder one's quest for enlightenment.)**

3. The New Age movement:

   a. Rejects sin as the ultimate cause of evil.
   b. Emphasizes personal autonomy.
   c. Accepts pantheism.
   d. (a) and (b)
   e. All of the above

4. In eastern spiritual meditation, a person is seeking to _____.

   a. pay for their sins
   b. vanish
   c. be resurrected
   d. hear God

5. The Bible teaches that Jesus Christ alone is the __**mediator**__ between
   the one, holy God and sinful human beings.

Witnessing Tips (Do's and Don'ts)

- *Do familiarize yourself with the basic teachings* of the type of Hinduism or Buddhism or teachings your friend follows.

- *Do ask questions* about your friend's personal beliefs (which may be different from what is commonly taught by their religious group).

- *Don't be quick to criticize your friend's religion* (or native culture) or engage in debates. You can encourage their trust and respect through personal kindness and your focus on Christ.

- *Do "be prepared to give an answer"* and explain "the reason for the hope that you have" (1 Peter 3:15). Know what you believe and why—and back it up from Scripture.

- *Don't overlook potentially sensitive cultural factors* that may be important to your friend, such as modest dress or a vegetarian diet.

- *Do share your personal testimony* of trusting in Christ for salvation. As appropriate, point your friend to the testimonies of Hindus/Buddhists/New Agers who have become Christians.

- *Do encourage your Hindu/Buddhist friend to read the Gospel of John* and be prepared to discuss it with him or her.

- *Do encourage New Age friends to read what the Bible says about Jesus* and clarify the meanings of scriptural terms (such as "Christ") that New Age writers commonly redefine.

- *Don't forget to pray faithfully* that God will draw your friend to Christ by the Holy Spirit.

The Dalai Lama

Tenzin Gyatso (1935–), the 14th Dalai Lama ("ocean of wisdom"), was born in rural Tibet. A monk of the Gelug ("Yellow Hat") sect of Tibetan Buddhism, he is said to be the reincarnation of the previous thirteen Dalai Lamas, the god-kings of Tibet (considered manifestations of Avalokitesvara, the bodhisattva of compassion). In 1959, he fled Tibet because of conflict with the ruling Chinese, and now heads the Tibetan government in exile in Dharamsala, India.

The Dalai Lama has done far more than anyone else to popularize Tibetan Buddhism in the West, cultivating well-publicized friendships with celebrities. But there is more to the story. In 2001 the Dalai Lama told an interviewer for Christianity Today that "Jesus Christ also lived previous lives," adding that Jesus "reached a high state, either as a Bodhisattva, or an enlightened person, through Buddhist practice or something like that."

In *A Guide to Cults and New Religions* (InterVarsity, 2005), researcher James Stephens notes that Tibetan Buddhism uses "a rigorous system of works righteousness" to enable followers to accumulate sufficient merit to "achieve deliverance from the … cycle of rebirths. These works include reciting mantras and sutras, … deity yoga, utilizing Buddhist rosary beads, prayer wheels, prayer flags and mani stones, visualizing demonic entities, and making symbolic offerings." Few people realize that the Dalai Lama's religion is also deeply occultic, thanks in part to the influence of the ancient Bön religion. The Dalai Lama consults the demon-possessed Nechung Oracle for state decisions, and the Tantrism of Tibetan Buddhism includes the ritual use of human remains and of bodily excretions known as the "five ambrosias."

(Adapted from *Christianity & Eastern Religions* Rose Publishing www.rose-publishing.com.)

Additional Resources

ℭ *Books*

The Illustrated Guide to World Religions by Dean C. Halverson (Bethany, 2003)

Neighboring Faiths: A Christian Introduction to World Religions by Winfried Corduan (InterVarsity, 1998)

Hinduism: A Brief Look at the Theology, History, Scriptures, and Social System with Comments on the Gospel in India by H.L. Richard (William Carey, 2007)

Chapatis for Tea: Loving Your Hindu Neighbour by Margaret Wardell and Ram Gidoomal (Highland, 1993)

Hinduism, TM and Hare Krishna by J. Isamu Yamamoto (Zondervan, 1998)

Sharing Your Faith With a Buddhist by Madasamy Thirumalai (Bethany, 2003)

Beyond Buddhism by J. Isamu Yamamoto (InterVarsity, 1982)

New Age Movement by Ron Rhodes (Zondervan, 1994)

ℭ *Internet*

South Asian Concern   www.southasianconcern.org

Karma to Grace   www.karma2grace.org

Sonrise Center for Buddhist Studies   www.sonrisecenter.org

World Religions: Comparative Analysis   www.comparativereligion.com

The inclusion of a work or web site does not necessarily mean endorsement of all its contents or of other works by the same author(s) or organization.

Islam

Session 6 Outline
Islam

1. Life of Muhammad

    a. Born in Mecca (AD 570)

    b. First encounter with Gabriel (AD 610)

    c. Journey to Medina (AD 622); Hijrah

    d. Conquest of Mecca (AD 630)

    e. Died in Medina (AD 632)

2. Scriptures and guiding documents

    a. The Qur'an

    b. The Bible—considered corrupted

    c. Sunnah (Hadith, Sira)

3. Six Beliefs

    a. Allah

    b. Prophets—including

    • Muhammad

    • Jesus

    c. Angels (and jinn)

    d. Holy books (Qur'an, Torah, Psalms, Gospels)

    e. Day of judgment

    f. Fate

4. Five Pillars

    a. Profession of faith (Shahadah)

    b. Prayers (Salat)

    c.   Almsgiving (Zakat)

    d.   Fasting (Sawm)

    e.   Pilgrimage to Mecca (Hajj)

5.   Salvation

    a.   No concept of original sin

    b.   Obedience through repentance and human effort

    c.   Two kinds of jihad

- Greater jihad (internal struggle to live a righteous life)

- Lesser jihad (holy war in defense of Islam)

6.   Three major expressions

    a.   Sunni

    b.   Shi'a

    c.   Sufi

    d.   Other expressions

- Folk Islam

- Islamism

- Jihadism

- Bahá'í Faith

- Nation of Islam

7.   The appeal of Islam

    a.   Simplicity of beliefs and requirements

    b.   Moral clarity

    c.   All-encompassing nature

    d.   Universal brotherhood

8. What does the Bible say?

    a. Romans 5:8

    b. 1 John 4:10

9. How to approach Muslims

    a. Be knowledgeable about Islam and Christianity

    b. Draw them out

    c. Emphasize Christianity is a relationship with God

    d. Be culturally sensitive

    e. Appreciate the high cost of leaving Islam

    f. Bear in mind that it's all about Muhammad

Key Terms

Arianism Originated in the fourth century AD and argues that Jesus does not share the same essence with God, and thus does not share in the same divine nature with eternity and authority. The Nicene, Chalcedonian, and Athanasian Creeds are primarily responses to this heresy.

Bahá'í Faith Founded in 1844 in Iran. Teaches that God has revealed himself through nine "manifestations" including Adam, Moses, Krishna, Buddha, Jesus, Muhammad, and Bahá'u'lláh. There are an estimated 8 million Bahá'ís worldwide.

Hadith A report of a saying or behavior of Muhammad which sets a precedent for Muslim practice and becomes the basis of shari'a.

Hajj The annual pilgrimage to Mecca.

Hijrah Muhammad's flight from Mecca to Medina in AD 622 which marks the first year in the Islamic calendar.

Injil The "book given to Jesus," similar to the Greek word *evangel*, meaning "good news." Muslims do not believe that no Injil remains on earth that hasn't been corrupted. Christians often refer to the Gospels, or a single Gospel, as "the Injil" when conversing with Muslims.

Islamism   Broad movement promoting the idea that full and correct implementation of Islam worldwide requires both political power and state control. Sometimes called fundamentalism or Salafism.

Jihad   ("holy fighting") A spiritual struggle that can either be internal (striving in one's soul to do right) or external (an effort against the enemies of Islam).

Jihadism   A radical Islamic ideology. It views Western democracy as a violation of tawheed and an offense to God, and creation of a perfect Islamic state by violent means as necessary.

Jinn   (also "Genie") A type of supernatural, personal being—distinct from humans and demons—said to have been made by Allah from smokeless fire. Jinn can be either helpful or harmful to mankind.

Kaaba (Ka'bah)   The cube-shaped structure in Mecca toward which all Muslims must pray. Believed to have been an altar used by Abraham.

Mecca   The center of idol worship in AD 610 when Muhammad first challenged the people to forsake idolatry and embrace Islam. Most Meccans rejected his message, and many began to persecute the early Muslims, causing them to flee (hijra) to the town of Medina in AD 622. Located in what is now Saudi Arabia.

Nation of Islam   Founded in 1930 in Detroit, Michigan by Wallace D. Fard. Currently led by Louis Farrakhan. Affirms belief in Allah and the Qur'an, but also teaches that millions of "Allahs" have lived and died since creation, and collectively the black race is God. Master Fard is considered the Supreme Allah and Savior.

Qur'an (Koran)   ("recitation") Revealed to Muhammad by the angel Gabriel over a period of 22 years. In AD 632 the recitations were collected together to become the Qur'an. Considered divine in its original Arabic.

Salat   A set ritual of prayer to be done five specific times every day (sometimes combined in three sessions), memorized in Arabic, with ritual washings before each sequence. The head must be covered, the body pointed toward Mecca, and the motions and prostrations must be followed for the prayers to be valid.

Shahadah   The foundational Muslim profession of faith: "There is no God but Allah, and Muhammad is his prophet."

Shari'a ("way," "path") Islamic religious law, based upon the Sunnah. The four schools of Sunni interpretation are named after their founders: Hanafi (d. 767), Maliki (d. 795), Shafi'i (d. 820), and Hanbali (d. 855). Shi'ia Muslims also have schools of their own.

Shi'a (Shi'ite) (from Arabic Shi'ati Ali, "party of Ali") A minority of Muslims (10% worldwide) which believes that the proper successor to Muhammad should be his blood relative, beginning with Ali, his son-in-law. The Sunni-Shi'a split happened shortly after Muhammad's death in a violent dispute about who should lead the Muslim community. Shi'a follow ten central practices which include the Five Pillars. Many believe in a series of 12 imams serving as Muhammad's spiritual and political successors. The final one will someday appear with Jesus.

Shirk ("associating") Committing blasphemy by assigning partners or equals to Allah, thereby compromising his uniqueness.

Sira (from Arabic Sirah Rasul Allah, "life of the messenger of God") Biographies of Muhammad that provide interpretive insights about his life and the early history of Islam.

Sufism A mystical form of Islam, often viewed as one of its distinct branches but which has both Sunni or Shi'a followers. Emphasis is placed on experiential knowledge of God, sometimes by trances induced through chanting the names of Allah or dancing (as seen in "whirling dervishes").

Sunnah Literally: the "trodden path" of Muhammad and his close companions. The Sunnah (Muhammad's examples) becomes the basis for shari'a.

Sunni (from Arabic Ahl as-Sunnah, "people of the tradition") The majority of Muslims (90% worldwide) identify themselves in contrast to the Shi'a. The Sunni-Shi'a split began shortly after Muhammad's death in a violent dispute about who should lead the Muslim community. Sunni hold to the Five Pillars and the Six Beliefs. Many believe that a figure from Muhammad's family, known as the Mahdi, will appear with Jesus before the final judgment.

Tawheed (Tawhid) ("oneness") The central doctrine of Allah's absolute oneness and uniqueness.

Before the Session

ℰ *Prepare:*

- Ask God for guidance and pray for each participant.

- Watch DVD Session 6 on your own.

- Review *Comparing Beliefs about the Afterlife* and *Witnessing Tips* on the following pages.

- See *Additional Resources* for further study.

- Read *Rose Bible Basics: Christianity, Cults & Religions* handbook chapter 4.

ℰ *Materials needed for this session:*

- DVD Session 6

- Bible

- Qur'an (optional)

- "Islam (Sunni & Shi'a)" section in *Christianity, Cults & Religions* PowerPoint® presentation (optional)

Opening the Session (5 minutes)

Use the *Did You Know?* facts to get participants thinking about today's topic. If you have a projector or whiteboard you can display the facts as participants enter the classroom. You can also read the facts aloud to the group before watching the DVD session.

When everyone gathers together, welcome participants and open the session in prayer. If you frequently have new participants joining the group, you may want to briefly cover the purposes of this learning about other religions and cults (see Session 1).

Did You Know?

- There are approximately 1.2 billion Muslims worldwide—90% of them are Sunni.
- Muslims consider Jesus a prophet of Allah and believe that he was born of a virgin and will come again someday.
- Muslims believe the Qur'an in Arabic is a copy of an eternal tablet in heaven.

Watch the DVD   SESSION 6 (35 minutes)

- Refer class members to the session outline in their Participant Guides for note taking.

Group Discussion (15 minutes)

If the class is large, divide participants into small groups. If time allows, have a spokesperson from each small group share with the rest of the class some of the insights discussed in their group. (These questions are also located in the Participant Guide.)

1. After watching this session, what did you learn about Islam that you didn't know or understand before?

2. Share about a time that you had an interaction or conversation with a Muslim. What did you learn from that experience?

3. How is salvation in Islamic teaching different than what Jesus taught about how to be saved?

4. How is the gospel of Jesus Christ good news for Muslims?

5. Read 1 Corinthians 9:19–23. How can you apply theses verses in your own conversations and interactions with Muslims?

Expand the Teaching (optional – 30 minutes)

To expand the session to 90 minutes use one or more of the following activities. (Activity sheets for participants are located in the Participant Guide.)

- **KEY BIBLE VERSES** This study in Scripture can be completed individually or in small groups.

- **QUICK QUIZ** The quiz is based on the content in the DVD session, so you will want to have participants complete it only after watching the DVD.

- **PRESENTATION** Teach through the "Islam (Sunni & Shi'a)" section in *Christianity, Cults & Religions* PowerPoint® presentation. Also see sections on "Bahai," and "Nation of Islam."

Reaching Out (5 minutes)

❡ *Encourage participants to do one or more of the following during the week:*

- Read carefully through *Witnessing Tips* in the Participant Guide.

- Reflect on these questions:

  1. What can I do to become more knowledgeable about Islam and Christianity?

  2. What steps can I take toward developing a relationship with someone I know who is a Muslim? How might God be leading me to one day share the gospel of grace with them?

  3. If I have only limited contact with Muslims, what can I do to support ministries or missionaries that reach out to Muslims?

(These questions are also found in the Participant Guide.)

❡ *Close the session in prayer.*

Key Bible Verses

ROMANS 8:15–17

"For you did not receive a spirit that makes you a slave again to fear, but you received the Spirit of sonship. And by him we cry, 'Abba, Father.' The Spirit himself testifies with our spirit that we are God's children. Now if we are children, then we are heirs—heirs of God and co-heirs with Christ, if indeed we share in his sufferings in order that we may also share in his glory." *NIV*

Q According to this passage, what is the result of receiving the "Spirit of sonship"?

A **We can call God "Abba, Father." We can be confident that we are God's children. We are co-heirs with Christ in suffering and in glory. We no longer need to be slaves to fear.**

HEBREWS 4:14–16

"Therefore, since we have a great high priest who has gone through the heavens, Jesus the Son of God, let us hold firmly to the faith we profess. For we do not have a high priest who is unable to sympathize with our weaknesses, but we have one who has been tempted in every way, just as we are—yet was without sin. Let us then approach the throne of grace with confidence, so that we may receive mercy and find grace to help us in our time of need." *NIV*

Q According to this passage, why can believers "approach the throne of grace with confidence"?

A **Because Jesus is our sinless high priest and the Son of God who sympathizes with us in our failings.**

ROMANS 5:8–10

"But God demonstrates his own love for us in this: While we were still sinners, Christ died for us. Since we have now been justified by his blood, how much more shall we be saved from God's wrath through him! For if, when we were God's enemies, we were reconciled to him through the death of his Son, how much more, having been reconciled, shall we be saved through his life!" *NIV*

1 JOHN 4:10

"This is love: not that we loved God, but that he loved us and sent his Son as an atoning sacrifice for our sins." *NIV*

Q   According to these two passages, on what do believers base their assurance that they will be saved from God's wrath?

A   **Because of Jesus' atoning sacrifice we are no longer enemies of God, but are now reconciled to the God who loves us!**

Quick Quiz   ANSWER KEY (Answers in Bold)

1. Which of the following is *not* taught in Islam?

   a. The Qur'an which people have today is a copy of an eternal tablet in heaven.

   b. The Torah, Psalms, and Gospels have been corrupted.

   c. **"Allah" refers to the Fatherhood of God. *(Allah is the generic word for God in Arabic. In Islam, Allah has no sons and cannot be associated with anything.)***

   d. Muhammad was the greatest man who ever lived.

2. True or False? The entire Qur'an was composed by Muhammad during the angel Gabriel's first visit. **FALSE *(The Qur'an was written by Muhammad over a period of 22 years.)***

3. Islam teaches that salvation depends upon:

   a. A person's good deeds outweighing their bad deeds.

   b. The will of Allah.

   c. **Both of the above *(A person's good works contribute to his or her salvation, but ultimately no one can know in advance what Allah will decide on the day of judgment.)***

   d. None of the above

4. True or False? In the final analysis Islam is all about Muhammad—what Muhammad says about God and what Muhammad would do in any situation. **TRUE**

5. Islam is a religion of works and merit, but according to the Bible, good works are the __**fruit (or outcome, result)**__ of salvation—not the means of attaining it.

Witnessing Tips   (Do's and Don'ts)

- *Do make it clear you are a follower of Christ,* by your loving words and righteous lifestyle.

- *Don't assume your Muslim friend understands what you mean* when you say "Christian."

- *Do take time to build a relationship.* Practice hospitality.

- *Don't be surprised if you are rejected at first.* It is best to offer Muslim friends store-bought sweets and to avoid anything with pork or alcohol.

- *Do approach your encounters as a learner.* Ask questions.

- *Don't take notes* and treat Muslim friends like an academic project.

- *Do correct their misunderstandings* of your beliefs.

- *Don't argue.* If they want to debate with a Christian, refer them to the web site www.debate.org.uk

- *Do talk about Jesus.* Use his title, Isa Al Masih.

- *Don't insult* the prophet Muhammad.

- *Do pray out loud with your Muslim friends.* Ask if you can pray for their practical needs, healing, and worries. Look for opportunities and pray in Jesus' name.

- *Don't start your prayer with "Our Father..."* because Muslims misunderstand the fatherhood of God (as sexual). Wait until you correct this misunderstanding before using "Father" or "Abba." At first address your prayer to "Almighty God" or "Lord God."

- *Do use your right hand* in giving and receiving gifts.

- *Don't use your left hand for eating food* (especially when learning to eat with your hands). The left hand is used for toilet cleaning; the right hand for eating.

- *Do treat your Bible with respect.* Store it high on a shelf. Some wrap it in a beautiful cloth.

- *Don't put your Bible on the floor or in the bathroom* as reading material. Many Muslims are superstitious about the bathroom.

- *Do be gender-sensitive:* interact man to man, woman to woman.

- *Don't allow any compromising situation,* even just to protect from a possible rumor. An Arab proverb says, "A man and woman alone together are three with the devil."

- *Do be careful with your body language.* Remove your shoes when entering a home or place of prayer (especially if you see shoes at the threshold).

- *Don't sit so that the sole of your foot or shoe is facing someone.* Women, don't look men directly in the eye, or at least quickly avert your glance.

- *Do practice modesty,* even among Westernized Muslims. For women this is especially important, since family honor is tied to their behavior and reputation.

- *Don't assume that Muslims think the same as you do,* even if they dress the same.

(Excerpt from *Islam & Christianity* Rose Publishing www.rose-publishing.com)

Comparing Beliefs about the Afterlife

	What Muslims Believe	**What Christians Believe**
Judgment Day	Everyone should fear judgment day, in which each person's deeds will be weighed on a scale. Each person has two "recording angels" who keep a list of every deed, both good and bad. Islamic teachers assign credits to deeds related to the pillars of Islam. It is unthinkable for many Muslims to abandon their accumulation of credits and trust a savior.	After death, all people await the final judgment when both believers and unbelievers will be resurrected. All will be judged according to the deeds they have done, but believers will be saved because God removed the record that contained the charges against them. He destroyed it by nailing it to the cross of Jesus (Colossians 2:14).
Salvation	In Islam, there is no savior. Salvation is possible, for Allah can always forgive (his will is supreme)—but he is primarily the judge. There are many descriptive warnings about hellfire and punishment in the Qur'an. Jihadists use the Qur'an to teach that paradise is guaranteed for their martyrs. Most Muslim scholars and leaders reject the terrorists' definitions of jihad and martyrdom.	Even if one's list of good deeds outweighed their list of bad deeds, it would not make them acceptable to God. The Bible says this would only cause boasting and pride, as though someone could impress God by their good deeds (Ephesians 2:8–10). Instead, God has credited believers with the righteousness of Christ, so salvation is a gift, not earned by anyone—not even martyrs—but bought with a great price (Jesus' blood).
Paradise	The Qur'an says, "For those who reject Allah, there is a terrible penalty: but for those who believe and work righteous deeds, there is forgiveness and a magnificent reward" (Surah 35:7). This great reward is janna, a garden paradise, an eternal place of both sensual and spiritual pleasures.	God the Father adopts those he saves into his family so they may live forever with Jesus in heaven. To be saved involves being "born again" into a new relationship with God (John 3:5).

(Adapted from *Islam & Christianity* Rose Publishing www.rose-publishing.com.)

Additional Resources

❧ *Books*

Answering Islam: The Crescent in Light of the Cross by Norman L. Geisler and Abdul Saleeb (Baker, 2002)

The Crisis of Islam: Holy War and Unholy Terror by Bernard Lewis (Random House, 2004)

Encountering the World of Islam, Keith E. Swartley, ed. (Authentic, 2005)

The Prophet & the Messiah: An Arab Christian's Perspective on Islam & Christianity by Chawkat Moucarry (InterVarsity, 2002)

Glad News! God Loves You, My Muslim Friend by Samy Tanagho (Authentic, 2004)

Knowing the Enemy: Jihadist Ideology and the War on Terror by Mary Habeck (Yale, 2006)

Muslims Next Door: Uncovering Myths and Creating Friendships by Shirin Taber (Zondervan, 2004)

Reasoning from the Scriptures with Muslims by Ron Rhodes (Harvest House, 2002)

❧ *Internet*

Muslim-Christian Debates   www.debate.org.uk

Answering Islam   www.answering-islam.org

❧ *DVD*

Christianity and Islam   (Vision Video, 2008)

The Cross or the Crescent: Understanding Islam   (NAMB, 2001)

More than Dreams   (Vision Video, 2007)

Behind the Sun   (Narrow Path, 1995)

❧ *More from Rose Publishing*

Islam & Christianity PowerPoint® (ISBN 9781596361324)

The inclusion of a work or web site does not necessarily mean endorsement of all its contents or of other works by the same author(s) or organization.

Other Products from Rose Publishing

Bible Reference Made Easy

Books, maps,
fold-out pamphlets,
Bible studies,
wall charts,
PowerPoint®
presentations

Hundreds of reproducible charts.

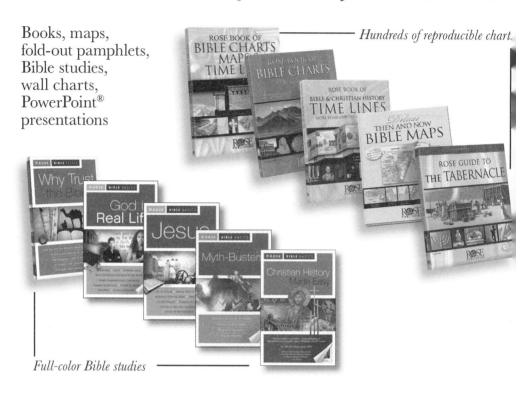

Full-color Bible studies

Fold-out pamphlets
These high-gloss plastic-coated
fact sheets contain hundreds of
facts and fit inside the cover of
most Bibles. They include the
most important information on
the topic at a glance.

Full-color wall charts

PUBLISHING

www.rose-publishing.com

Found wherever good Christian books are sold